The National Forensic League Honor Society promotes secondary school speech and debate activities and interscholastic competition as a means to develop a student's lifelong skills and values, as well as the public's awareness of the value of speech, debate, and communication education.

The organization serves as the central agent for coordination and facilitation of:

- heightened public awareness of the value of speech communication skills;
- development of educational initiatives for student and teacher training;
- excellence in interscholastic competition;
- the promotion of honor society ideals.

As an organization, the National Forensic League embraces diversity, interconnection, and visionary leadership. The National Forensic League empowers students to become effective communicators, ethical individuals, critical thinkers, and leaders in a democratic society.

To learn more about starting a National Forensic League or National Junior Forensic League program at the middle or high school level, or to locate more resources on speech and/or debate, please contact National Forensic League, 125 Watson Street, Ripon, WI 54971, (920) 748-6206, or visit our Web site at **www.nflonline.org**.

Contents

Chapter 1   *The History of Lincoln-Douglas Debate*   *6*

Chapter 2   *The Structure of an LD Debate*   *10*

Chapter 3   *The Format of LD Debate*   *20*

Chapter 4   *Persuasive Writing and Speaking*   *34*

Chapter 5   *Doing Your Research*   *38*

Chapter 6   *Tips for Debate . . . and Life!*   *43*

Glossary   *46*

For More Information   *47*

For Further Reading   *47*

Bibliography   *47*

Index   *48*

Chapter 1

The History of Lincoln-Douglas Debate

Abraham Lincoln and Stephen Douglas debated in 1858 when the two men were campaigning for one of the Illinois seats in the U.S. Senate. The debates were not just about whether slavery should be legal, but about issues surrounding the practice of slavery. Both Lincoln and Douglas agreed slavery was a problem for the country, but disagreed on how it should be resolved. Douglas believed those kinds of decisions should be left to the local community and state, while Lincoln believed the national government should make those decisions. As you can see, the debate was about more than slavery. It was about who had the power to make the decision.

Lincoln and Douglas Go Head-to-Head

Although the language of that time was a bit different from how we speak today, we can see in Lincoln's and Douglas's language the beginnings of the Lincoln-Douglas Debate format we know today. In one debate, Lincoln stated: "I should like to know, if taking this old Declaration of Independence, which declares that all men are equal upon principle, and making exceptions to it, where will it stop? If one man says it does not mean a Negro, why may not another man say it does not mean another man? If that declaration is not the truth, let us get this statute book in which we find it and tear it out."

To this, Stephen Douglas responded: "There you find that Mr. Lincoln told the Abolitionists of Chicago that if the Declaration of Independence did not declare that the Negro was created by the Almighty the equal of the white man, that you ought to take that instrument and tear out the clause which says that all men were created equal . . . .You know that in his Charleston speech, an extract from which he has read, he declared that the Negro belongs to an inferior race; is physically inferior to the white man, and should always be kept in an inferior position." Douglas was explaining that he thought Lincoln was contradicting himself and tried to persuade the audience that Lincoln wasn't sticking to one side or the other.

Until 1913, each state's legislature elected the men who would represent the state in the Senate, so it was unusual for Lincoln and Douglas to have these debates in front of everyday citizens. However, they decided that it was important for the public to understand what they thought and valued, even if the public didn't elect the senators. Douglas defeated Lincoln and was reelected to the Senate in 1858. However, these public debates gave Lincoln contact with the people and helped him get elected to the presidency in 1860. The appeal of the Lincoln-Douglas debates to a common audience gave this form of debate its place in history and made it a popular type of debate in schools everywhere.

Today's Lincoln-Douglas Debate

Today, the format of Lincoln-Douglas Debate is similar to the format used by Abraham Lincoln and Stephen Douglas. One speaker begins with a prepared statement and the other speaker responds. The speakers then take turns answering one another's arguments.

Lincoln-Douglas Debates are about topics—or "resolutions"—that are predetermined and given to the debaters far in advance. Resolutions are statements of fact which one debater tries to prove true and the other tries to prove false. Resolutions change every 2 months with some overlap time, giving debaters at least 2 weeks to prepare cases on both sides. Most resolutions are related to social values in some way—they don't just ask how the government should act, but how people should act with each other.

The most important thing to remember about any resolution is that the debaters are not trying to prove the government should take a certain action, as in policy debate. Instead, Lincoln-Douglas Debates try to prove that something is generally true or false. For example, if the resolution states that "society ought to have a strict separation of church and state," debaters don't need to prove how the strict separation of church and state would happen. Instead, both debaters just need to talk about whether there should be a separation, and why.

Abraham Lincoln (left) challenged Stephen Douglas to a series of seven debates. The first debate took place in Ottawa, Illinois.

9

Chapter 2

The Structure of an LD Debate

Lincoln-Douglas Debate, or "LD debate," is one-on-one, meaning that each student debates against only one other student in each debate. The affirmative debater's job is to prove the resolution is true. The negative debater's job is to prove the resolution is false.

In Lincoln-Douglas Debate, each debater learns to argue both sides of a resolution. At the beginning of a debate, each debater reads a constructive case, presenting his or her major arguments in support of or against the topic. A Lincoln-Douglas case is structured very much like a persuasive speech with an introduction, body, and conclusion. One of the more important elements of a Lincoln-Douglas case is the use of a goal or value that is important to protect and which your arguments support. This is called a value premise, and it's the basis of LD's reputation as "value debate."

Let's see how each argument—or case—in the debate is structured.

Lincoln-Douglas Debate

Cynthia Woodhouse

The National Forensic League · Library of Public Speaking and Debate

rosen publishing's
rosen
central®

New York

For my father, Paul H. Woodhouse. His unconditional support and sacrifice cannot be measured with money or expressed in words, but are appreciated with love.

Published in 2007 by The Rosen Publishing Group, Inc.
29 East 21st Street, New York, NY 10010

First Edition

Library of Congress Cataloging-in-Publication Data

Woodhouse, Cynthia.
  Lincoln-Douglas debate / Cynthia Woodhouse.
     p. cm. - (The National Forensic League library of public speaking and debate)
  Includes bibliographical references and index.
  ISBN-13: 978-1-4042-1025-7
  ISBN-10: 1-4042-1025-3 (library binding)
  1. Lincoln-Douglas debates, 1858. 2. Debates and debating. I. Title.
  E457.4.W66 2007
  973.6'8-dc22
                              2006033655

Manufactured in the United States of America

Criterion	In order to determine which position in today's round best provides opportunity for self-actualization, the affirmative proposes the criterion of participation. This means that the individual has the best opportunity to interact with society regardless of the type of governing system in place. This criterion is important to the value of self-actualization because, without the ability to interact meaningfully with society, the individual will be unable to determine for himself or herself what is beneficial and what isn't.
Thesis	Oppressive government is better than no government because it provides social interaction better than an absence of government, and that ultimately leads to self-actualization for the individual.
Contention Taglines (These are just taglines. Actual contentions explain a lot more.)	Contention One: Democracy is more readily achieved from oppression than from anarchy. Contention Two: Democracy leads to better self-actualization.

Chapter 3

The Format of LD Debate

In Lincoln-Douglas Debate, each side is allowed to question the other side's case and try to disprove it. This is done in a formal way.

A typical debate round gives both speakers the same amount of time (13 minutes) to present their arguments and explain why their opponent's arguments are not true. Cross-examination time isn't included in the 13 minutes each debater must speak, since the length of each cross-examination period depends on how long it takes each opponent to either ask or answer questions. Thus, it's not guaranteed speaking time for one side or the other. Either the judge or a specially appointed timekeeper should be watching the time and signal to the debaters how much time they have remaining in each speech. It's still a good idea for each debater to have their own timer to keep track of time.

Here is the format:

First Affirmative Constructive (1AC)	6 minutes
Cross-Examination (Negative asks Affirmative)	3 minutes
First Negative Constructive (1NC)	7 minutes
Cross-Examination (Affirmative asks Negative)	3 minutes
First Affirmative Rebuttal (1AR)	4 minutes
First Negative Rebuttal (1NR)	6 minutes
Second Affirmative Rebuttal (2AR)	3 minutes

First Affirmative Constructive: The Affirmative States Their Case

The debate begins with the affirmative standing to read their prepared speech, which is 6 minutes long and is called the first affirmative constructive (1AC). The affirmative uses this speech to present their arguments to the audience without anyone interrupting. During this time, the negative debater and the audience write down key information to help them remember what the affirmative has said.

Cross-Examination: The Negative Asks Questions

Once the affirmative finishes their prepared speech, they remain standing and the negative stands to ask questions. This 3-minute period is called cross-examination. The negative could ask questions to clarify things they didn't understand about the affirmative case or to find problems with it.

Let's see how two imaginary debaters—let's call them Kasey and Michelle—might do cross-examination. In this imaginary case, the resolution is that the government should provide health care to its citizens. Kasey (K) is the affirmative and has just finished reading her prepared speech. Michelle (M), the negative, will be asking her questions:

Michelle (M)

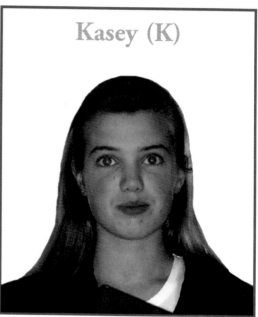

Kasey (K)

M—Could you please repeat what you said your criterion was?

K—My criterion is equity.

M—And what is equity?

K—Equity is impartiality and equal access.

M—Okay, thanks. How do you define justice?

K— Justice is fairness, goodness, and equity. A just government would protect rights.

M—So equity is a basic principle of justice?

K— Yes.

M—Do all people benefit equally from health care?

K— They could or they couldn't. It's an implementation problem. Regardless of whether they actually do or don't, I still say that a just government should provide health care.

M—So, if people benefit in different ways from health care, isn't that a violation of equity?

K— No.

M—Why not?

K— Every person has the equitable ability to receive health care, not just some people.

M—Without governmental provision of health care, do all people lose the basic right of subsistence and die?

K— No. Not all people, but there will be some who suffer, and it's the responsibility of the government to prevent as much suffering as possible.

Notice that Michelle starts by asking Kasey to repeat something she didn't get written down at the beginning of Kasey's case, then asks some other questions to help clarify exactly what Kasey meant by some of her other arguments.

After the negative asks questions, they can take some

time to prepare for their upcoming speech. Each side has 3 minutes of preparation time for the entire debate. This means that debaters need to be careful about when they use this time. The negative usually spends 1 to $1\frac{1}{2}$ minutes before the negative constructive, planning what they want to say against the affirmative.

First Negative Constructive

The negative's first speech, called the first negative constructive (1NC), has a lot to cover in 7 short minutes. First, the negative reads their prepared speech. This should only take about 4 minutes to read and can be as short as 3 minutes. Once the prepared speech has been read, the negative talks about the affirmative's arguments, starting with the value premise and criterion. Again, the value premise, or simply "value," is the most important goal of the debate. The value criterion, or simply "criterion," is the way in which a debater achieves their value.

The negative should explain why their value is more appropriate to the resolution and why their criterion is better for achieving it. After that, the negative should look at each of the main arguments—or contentions—the affirmative made and explain one at a time why they're not true. As much as possible, the negative should try to answer what the affirmative said using arguments from the negative constructive. At the end of the speech, the negative should give a conclusion that summarizes their case and the reasons the affirmative case isn't true.

In our imaginary debate, Michelle starts by talking about Kasey's value and criterion before talking about the main argument Kasey makes. Because Kasey's case is pretty simple and focused on just one thing, Michelle talks about it as one major argument.

"Now that my case has been established, let's talk about some problems with my opponent's case. The first problem with her case is her criterion. She says justice is based in equity, or equal treatment of people. This is a problem because all people in a society aren't the same. They have different needs, interests, and goals. These disparities make treating everyone equally nearly impossible.

"Her only contention is that health care is a basic right that helps to support the natural right to life; however, this doesn't directly relate to why a government should provide it. Remember, my own argument says that there are two parts of any society: the government and the producers. This means that the people are responsible for producing goods and services and the government is simply meant to make and enforce laws."

The Affirmative Cross-Examination

Following the negative's speech, the affirmative gets a chance to ask the negative questions not only about the negative case, but also about arguments the negative made against the affirmative case. The affirmative should try to clear up as much as they can so they can prepare good reasons why the negative side and the responses against the affirmative are not true.

In our imaginary debate, see how Kasey doesn't give up when she keeps getting confusing answers from Michelle:

K— What is justice?

M—Justice is the harmonious balance of part and whole.

K— And what does that mean?

M—It means that the different parts of society have to perform their prescribed roles.

K— So if I'm a murderer, is it just for me to continue murdering?

M—No. As a member of society, you have a role as a producer. There is no prescribed role in society for murderers.

K— If I am fulfilling my role in society, I am just.

M—Yes.

K— What is the role of a government?

M—To provide law.

K— Why is that what the government is supposed to do and nothing else?

M—Because that's the only purpose of a government.

K— But why?

M—Because the government is a special group of people who have that specific job. The other people in society give the power to make and enforce laws to one group and agree to split the rest of the work as producers.

K— So who provides health care?

M—The doctor. The doctor is a member of the producer class.

K— Okay. No more questions.

Once the affirmative has asked questions, they may want to take some preparation time to decide what they want to say against the negative case. Typically, the affirmative takes $1\frac{1}{2}$ to 2 minutes before their next speech.

First Affirmative Rebuttal

The third speech in the debate is the first affirmative rebuttal (1AR). This speech is only 4 minutes long, but there is a lot to be done! Before speaking, the affirmative needs to decide the most important arguments. Should they start by rebuilding their own case or by responding to the arguments in the negative case? Once the affirmative decides, they should begin speaking, making arguments from the beginning of one case to the end.

For example, if the affirmative thinks there are more important arguments on the affirmative side, they will begin at the top of the affirmative case. The first thing the affirmative needs to talk about is why their own value is better than the negative's value and why the negative's response against the affirmative's value isn't true. The affirmative will then do the same with responses the negative made against the criterion and each of the main arguments.

Next, the affirmative goes to the negative case and makes arguments against what the negative said—beginning with the value and criterion—and moving on to the negative's main arguments. The affirmative should try to spend 2 minutes on each argument to be sure they are answering the most important arguments on each side. At the end of the speech, the affirmative needs to offer a conclusion that summarizes what they've proven. In our imaginary debate, Kasey starts by summarizing what Michelle's case says before talking about Michelle's responses to the affirmative. Let's look at page 28 to see how she does this.

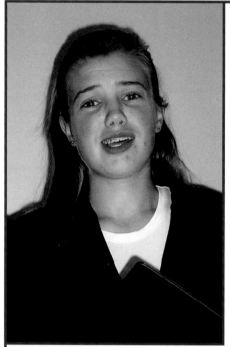

"My opponent says my criterion of equity isn't good because people have different needs. She says justice is better defined as the harmonious balance of part and whole. However, while a government does need to perform its own job of making laws, the government also needs to be sure it provides for all of its people equally and protects the rights of all people. This means my criterion of equity is better because it shows how a government should perform its duties.

"This also means my opponent's case helps support mine. She says that a government has a specific role, but I contend that the role of government is to protect the rights of the people. Because health care protects the right to life, it is the government's responsibility to provide health care.

"So let's look at why my affirmative case is still true. I say a government must protect the rights of the people—including the right to life—in order to be just. Health care is a basic right because it directly affects the right to life and the quality of that life. Providing health care is the best way to protect the right to life because it maintains a positive energy for the people. When the government provides health care, the quality of life is protected equally. Therefore, a just government should provide health care to its citizens."

First Negative Rebuttal

The negative now has a chance to take the rest of their preparation, or prep, time to get ready for their final speech of the debate. Remember, even though the negative only gets to speak twice, they get 13 minutes total (7 in the first speech, 6 in the second), the same amount as the affirmative. Once the negative has taken some time to prepare for their last speech, they need to make the same decisions the affirmative made: which arguments are most important? This final negative speech is called the first negative rebuttal (1NR). In 6 minutes, the negative needs to answer arguments the affirmative made against the negative case, make more arguments against the affirmative case, and give reasons why the negative should win the debate.

The negative can begin with either the affirmative or the negative case when making responses. However, the negative needs to be very clear about which case they are starting with. Often, negatives begin with the negative case and explain why the affirmative's responses against the negative case aren't true and why the negative's original arguments are still true. Then the negative addresses the affirmative case, explaining once more why the main affirmative arguments are not true and answering the responses the affirmative made in their last speech. The negative needs to explain again why their value is still most appropriate for the resolution and why their criterion is the best way to achieve it.

In our imaginary debate, Michelle chooses to start with the affirmative case before moving on to the negative. Let's look at page 30 to see how she does this.

"In my last speech, I said a government can't provide for things based on the principle of equity because people will always have different needs and wants. If the government provides health care to the people, it won't be equal because people will need and use it differently.

"All my opponent really tells you in her case is that the government should protect the rights of the people, but she never explains why this means the government should provide health care. The reason the government shouldn't provide health care is because even if a government should act equally toward all of its people, it still only has to make and enforce laws. The rest of the people are the producers, which means they have the responsibility of filling in the 'holes' the government doesn't cover. The doctor in society has the job of providing health care services to the people.

"The affirmative's main attack on my case is that the government should protect the rights of the people and should do what it can to protect the right to life. This may be true. However, the police have the job of making sure the laws are being enforced and the job of the government is to make the laws that the police enforce. The job of the rest of the people in society is then to provide for health care because they are the producers. So, you should vote for the negative because I have proven that while the government should provide equally for the people, this is impossible in terms of health care because people have such different needs. A government shouldn't provide health care to its citizens. The producers in a society should provide health care."

Voting Issues

Once the negative has talked specifically about the negative and affirmative cases, the negative will need time to give two or three reasons why they've won the debate. These are called "voting issues." The negative should spend 2 minutes on the negative case, 2 minutes on the affirmative case, and have 2 minutes to explain what the major issues are and why they've won.

The first thing the negative should address in these voting issues is the value and criterion debate. The negative should specifically explain why their value is the most important and why their criterion is the best way to achieve it. From there, the negative needs to resummarize their own position. They should explain why their major arguments are not only true, but how and why these arguments relate to their value and criterion and prove the resolution false. The negative also needs some kind of concluding statement, such as "and that's why you negate" or "so _____(resolution) is not true."

In our imaginary debate, Michelle talks about all of this at once. She says her case is better, then concludes with a major reason why the resolution isn't true. In this case, Michelle doesn't separate the voting issue from the rest of the speech. That's fine, because she makes it clear that the argument she's talking about is the most important one.

Second Affirmative Rebuttal

Before the second affirmative rebuttal (2AR)—which is the final speech of the debate and lasts only 3 minutes—the affirmative needs to decide which arguments are the most important. They then use their prep time to decide which arguments will take up most of the time in the final rebuttal. The affirmative should take the rest of their prep time to prepare a complete "story" about what's going to win the debate. A "story" in debate should begin with the value and criterion and explain why the affirmative's side is better and more appropriate for the resolution. After that, the affirmative should explain why their arguments show how they've met the criterion and how this relates to the value and proves the resolution true. Then the affirmative should talk about how their arguments are still true and how they've met the criterion and value. The final statement of the affirmative should be short, to the point, and summarize the most important reason the affirmative has won the debate.

"Enacting legislation is the same thing as providing for rights, so if the government enacts legislation to provide for the rights of the people, it is acting justly. This means that if I can prove that a government can enact legislation to provide health care to its citizens, then it should provide health care to its citizens. From the beginning of the debate, I have been arguing that a just government should enact legislation as its primary job. However, the difference between my opponent and me is that I say the legislation should include looking at the needs of the people, which means the government should provide health care for its citizens."

In our imaginary debate, the affirmative spends most of her time explaining what a government is supposed to do, since that's what most of the debate has focused on up to this point.

At the end of this debate, the affirmative spends a bit more time explaining that her position is a lot like her opponent's in several ways, but that the key difference is the reason the judge should vote for her. Notice that the affirmative ends her final speech with a statement of the resolution on her side to help remind the audience what she is arguing for and what the resolution was. Both debaters have now made their arguments, responded to one another, and summarized their major "clash." Now it's up to the judge or audience to decide who was more persuasive!

Chapter 4

Persuasive Writing and Speaking

The easiest way to write a complete argument is in the *claim, warrant, data, impact* format. A claim is a controversial statement, or a statement people could disagree with. It is the simplest statement of the argument. Following the claim is the warrant. A warrant is the reason why the argument is true. The warrant should be the debater's own explanation about the argument, giving a reason why the audience should believe it. Next is the data. Data is information from a published, credible author that supports the claim the debater is making. It can be a direct quotation or a summary of a study the author conducted to help prove the point. The final part of the argument is the impact. An impact is a reason why the argument is important. The impact should relate back to the value and criterion in some way and help prove the thesis true.

The terms "claim," "warrant," "data," and "impact" should not be used in writing the case. Instead, an argument should be structured using transition sentences like the ones shown below. Instead of using the words on the left, use the sentences on the right:

Claim	"My first argument is . . . ."
Warrant	"The reason this is true is . . . ."
Data	"This is supported by (author name) when they say . . . ."
Impact	"This is important because . . . ."

Writing the Conclusion

After each main argument has been presented, the case needs a conclusion. A good conclusion begins by restating the thesis statement exactly as it was stated at the beginning of the case. Next, the debater restates each main argument by restating the taglines. Finally, the concluding statement should be persuasive and eloquent, but it should also relate back to the attention-getter at the beginning of the case. Following this structure, a debater tells the audience what they're going to tell them, then tells the audience what they've told them. This may seem repetitive, but the repetition actually helps the audience remember the arguments more easily.

Ethos, Pathos, and Logos

When speaking or writing to convince someone of a point, there are many things to consider. Each audience will be different and won't necessarily be persuaded by the same things. To write and speak so people will agree with you, there are three persuasive approaches to consider—ethos, pathos, and logos.

35

Ethos is the ability to say and write things that show you know what you're talking about. It's important that the audience believes and trusts the speaker and is willing to accept what they're saying. To achieve this, the debater needs to be well read on the subject so they can speak about it confidently. The debater also needs to have good evidence to support what they're saying. The debater can show they care what the audience thinks by using examples that relate to the audience's experience, incorporating everyday examples the audience will understand and appreciate.

Pathos is the manipulation of and appeal to the audience's emotions. Think of television commercials, like those for greeting cards. Commercials try to connect with their audience by making them think of something that means a lot to them or by showing people and pictures that make the audience feel happy or sad. In the same way, debaters need to "sell" their arguments to their audience. The debater also needs to speak in an interesting way, using inflection to highlight some of the case's more important words and phrases.

Using emotional words and examples makes the audience identify with the argument, which will make them more likely to believe it. Debaters need to be careful not to overdo it, though. They should avoid bringing up controversial issues and instead use examples that are more predictable and subtle, such as how angry someone might be if a thief stole their CDs.

Logos is logic and reasoning. Before a speaker begins, they need to decide how to best communicate their message logically to their particular audience. For instance, you would more easily convince your parents that you needed a new computer if you could prove it would help you with your schoolwork and you would thus get better grades.

Know Your Audience

Different communities have differ-ent beliefs and values and, as times change, so do these beliefs. When circumstances change in society, some ideas might be more acceptable than others.

Debaters always have to consider how to communicate with a specific audience, in a specific place, at a spe-cific time. They need to consider what's going on in the community, state, nation, or world and how those events may affect people's feelings about government, politics, current events, or other cultures. How a debater presents an argument to their classmates should be different from how they present an argument to a group of adults—these two groups understand things differently and relate to different kinds of exam-ples. Debaters should always be aware of the people they are trying to persuade and think about what those people might believe (are they more conservative or liber-al?) and things they might prefer not to hear (jokes about a certain president might not be well received).

Chapter 5

Doing Your Research

Before starting to write a debate case, each debater needs to read as much as possible on the topic. This helps the debater find out what people are saying about the topic or similar issues. However, researching can be tricky if you don't know where to look, especially when the topic seems complex. There are a lot of places a debater can look to do research.

Books are a great place to begin and can give the debater a starting point to work from. Magazines, newspapers, and journals are also full of useful information, as is the Internet. The trick is to get creative in your research—finding just the right quotation or statistic can make the difference between a good case and a great case. Use your imagination!

Crack the Books

School, public, and university and college libraries may have extensive collections of books on current events, government, history, and many other useful topics. Debaters should start with their school libraries. Talk to a librarian to find helpful sources. Often, a librarian will have search tips that offer other ways to find information beyond the words and phrases in the resolution. Debaters should also go to the public library, which will often have more books about a certain subject. University and college libraries may have the widest selection of resources.

When searching through book resources, the debater should go in with a list of search words that go beyond the specific words in the resolution. For example, for the resolution "An oppressive government is better than no government," the debater should be ready to search the following terms:

- oppression
- government
- tyranny (an oppressive government)
- anarchy (a form of society where there is no government)
- the state (a political body ruled by government)
- chaos

Debaters should get creative with their search terms. In addition to using the above terms to look through card catalogs and digital databases, debaters should go to the index of a book to see if any of their search terms appear there. The index will list major subject areas addressed in the book and page numbers where they are referenced. Debaters should also consult the table of contents to see if anything relates to the topic.

Periodicals

Periodicals are magazines, newspapers, journals, and other publications that come out more than once a year. Again, be prepared with many different search terms, not just the ones mentioned in the resolution. Many schools and public libraries have access to an Internet database known as EBSCOhost, which gives access to all kinds of magazine and newspaper articles. If your school or public library doesn't have access to this database, suggest it!

The Internet

Now that almost everyone has access to the Internet, research has gotten easier. Debaters need to remember, however, that not everything on the Internet is valuable information. The first thing all Internet surfers need to know is that the letters at the end of a Web address—called "extensions"— actually mean something. The chart on page 41 lists some of the most common extensions and what they mean.

Extension	What It Means	Reason to Be Careful
.com	This is a commercial extension. Anyone can own this type of Web site because it's open space that has been bought or rented.	Anyone can own one. A scientist could have written the information on the page, or a college student, or the kid down the block. It's information you should definitely double-check.
.gov	This is a government Web site. The only people who can post or change things on these sites are government employees. The most common Web sites with this ending are departments of the government, like the Department of Homeland Security.	The information comes from the viewpoint of whoever is running the government at the time. Information on these sites when a Republican is in office may be very different from that when a Democrat is in office.
.edu	These sites are education-related. The Web sites are controlled and updated by schools or school-related services like colleges and universities.	The information may reflect the school or educational institution posting it. The beliefs and values of that school will probably affect the information on the site.
.org	This site relates to a registered organization of some kind. Most nonprofit organizations have a Web site with this ending.	These sites are posted and changed by organizations, so the information will probably be biased toward the organization's point of view. Debaters should read the information carefully and decide if it seems true or exaggerated to further the organization's causes.

In addition to general Web sites and library-supported search engines, here are some others that can give specialized information.

http://www.newsbank.com	http://www.unitedstreaming.com
One of the best, this database provides access to a number of school, college and university, local, national, government, and global publications.	This is a database where debaters can search for digital video, clips, and images for streaming and downloading.
http://online.culturegrams.com	http://library.cqpress.com/cqresearcher
This site gives information about the cultures of 182 countries. Entries include maps, statistics, information on history, people, customs, lifestyles, and society. It gives photos, recipes, and national anthems.	This site has articles on many different subjects, including social issues such as the environment, health, education, science, and technology. Articles are updated weekly.
http://infotrac.galegroup.com	http://firstsearch.oclc.org
This is a great site that covers literature, authors, biography, science, and history.	This site is a collection of ten databases: ArticleFirst, ECO, ERIC, GPO Monthly Catalog, Medline, PapersFirst, ProceedingsFirst, UnionLists, WorldAlmanac, and WorldCat.

These Web sites require subscriptions and are username/password-protected. A school can get a subscription to these online databases for a yearly fee. In some instances, the state may already provide or may consider providing funding for subscriptions to one or more of these databases for a public or school library. These are great resources for all classes and activities.

If a Web page does not show an author's name, you can look at a Web site called www.register.com. Doing a "WHOIS" search and entering the Web address will show the person, company, or organization responsible for the site's content. This can help you decide if the information is going to be useful or biased.

Chapter 6

Tips for Debate . . . and Life!

Lincoln-Douglas Debate is a full presentation. It isn't just based on what the debaters say, but how they say it and what they look like when they're talking. If you've ever seen someone give a speech to a large audience, they were most likely dressed up. Dressing nicely when addressing a large audience shows that the same amount of time and attention the speaker put into their speech was also put into their appearance. A speaker who is dressed appropriately will seem more believable to an audience because they not only sound good, they look good, too!

Debaters need to not only consider how they're dressed, but also their posture, the way they talk, and how they treat their opponents. Here are some tips for presenting yourself as professionally as possible.

Dress for Success

When engaging in debate in class or in competition, the debater should wear clothes that are clean and pressed. Ideally, men will be wearing suits with jackets and pants, as well as ties. However, suits can be expensive. Some alternatives are: khaki pants or dress pants, a matching collared dress shirt, a tie, a belt, dark socks, and dress shoes. Ladies should consider a skirt, neutral stockings, and closed-toe shoes.

Debaters should also be well groomed. Hair should be clean and neat, makeup should be tasteful, and jewelry should be kept simple. The debater's overall appearance should be clean, organized, and well planned.

It's All in the Presentation

When speaking to an audience, debaters need to be aware of their vocal inflection, posture, and volume. They should always be standing to help project their voices throughout the room and to support good breathing. They should stand with their feet firmly planted so they aren't tempted to sway back and forth or shift their weight.

A debater's posture should be comfortable but professional. When a debater is reading information from their case or from their notes later in the debate, they should hold the paper in one hand slightly off to the side so they can gesture with the other hand and keep from relying too much on the written text. Eye contact is also important. The debater should be sure they are talking to the audience, not at the audience, and should try to keep eye contact with each person in the audience for 3 to 5 seconds.

Finally, the debater's speaking volume should be proportional to the size of the room and to the debater's distance from the audience. In a typical classroom, the debater can speak at a conversational volume. If the room is smaller, the debater can lower their volume a bit. If a debate is in a large lecture hall, the debater should speak louder (but not too loud), especially if audience members are sitting further back in the hall.

Be a Good Competitor!

Lincoln-Douglas Debate is a great way to meet new people and sharpen your own arguments and conversation skills. This competition is more fun when everyone has the opportunity to compete fairly and in a positive environment. You should always treat your opponent and audience with respect, as you would expect them to treat you. Other debaters may have more or less experience than you, but it's important to simply do your best.

Being a good competitor means being gracious both when you win and when you lose. Regardless of the debate's outcome or your opinion of your opponent's skill level, you should never criticize your opponent, members of the audience, or the judge. Your job as a debater is to do your best to persuade your audience to believe what you're saying, which won't necessarily be interpreted the same way by your audience. What you can learn from each and every debate is what that particular audience found to be persuasive or true and what they didn't. You can learn new ideas and new ways of thinking from your opponent. Most importantly, by engaging in any kind of debate, you can learn more about yourself, your own beliefs and knowledge, and how they relate to the world around you. Debate is a fun way to prepare you for life!

Glossary

affirmative The person in favor of the resolution.

conservative Believing in maintaining existing views, conditions, or practices.

criterion The standard that is presented by a debater to illustrate the relative importance of a value. The judge uses the criterion to judge the round.

format The plan or arrangement of something.

impartiality Treating both sides in a debate equally.

inflection The change in pitch or loudness of a person's voice.

judge The person who makes the final decision about who wins the round.

liberal Believing in challenging existing views, conditions, or practices.

manipulation To control something to one's own advantage.

negate To deny the truth of.

negative The person against the resolution.

predetermined Decided on beforehand.

rebuttal Speech designed to refute the other person's position and arguments. In a rebuttal, a speaker tries to disprove the opponent's case and defends their own.

resolution The actual word-for-word statement of the topic that the affirmative must support and the negative must prove false.

statistic A fact that gives information, usually in the form of numbers.

statute A law.

subscription The right to receive something for a period of time because you have paid for it.

timer The device every judge must bring to the round to keep track of the speaking times. This can be a digital stopwatch, a kitchen timer, or a watch.

transition A sentence that guides a discussion from one subject to another.

For More Information

Debate Central
NCPA Headquarters
12770 Coit Road, Suite 800
Dallas, TX 75251 • (972) 386-6272
http://www.debate-central.org

Lincoln-Douglas Education Project
Hobart & William Smith Colleges
Scandling Center, Box 4136
Geneva, NY 14456 • (315) 781-3182
http://people.hws.edu/barnes/ldep/index.html

The National Association of Urban Debate Leagues
332 S. Michigan Avenue, Suite 500
Chicago, IL 60604 • (312) 427-8101
http://www.urbandebate.org

National Forensic League
125 Watson Street
P.O. Box 38
Ripon, WI 54971 • (920) 748-6206
http://www.nflonline.org

Web Sites

Due to the changing nature of Internet links, the Rosen Publishing Group, Inc., has developed an online list of Web sites related to the subject of this book. This site is updated regularly. Please use this link to access the list: **http://www.rosenlinks.com/psd/ldde**

For Further Reading

Angle, Paul M., ed. *The Complete Lincoln-Douglas Debates of 1858*. Chicago, IL: University of Chicago Press, 1991.

Bennet, William H. *Beginning Debate*. Taos, NM: Championship Debate Enterprises, 2003.

Davidson, Josephine. *The Middle School Debater*. Bellingham, WA: Right Book Co., 1997.

Meany, John, and Kate Shuster. *Speak Out! Debate and Public Speaking in the Middle Grades*. New York: IDEA Press, 2005.

Phillips, Leslie, William S. Hicks, and Douglas R. Springer. *Basic Debate*. New York: Glencoe/McGraw-Hill, 2005.

Sather, Trevor. *Pros and Cons: A Debater's Handbook*. London, United Kingdom: Routledge, 1999.

Bibliography

Black, Henry, ed. *Black's Law Dictionary Abridged,* 6th ed. St. Paul, MN: The West Group, 1991.

Brainy Quote: Henry A. Kissinger Quotes
http://www.brainyquote.com/quotes/authors/h/henry_a_kissinger.html

Excerpts from the Lincoln-Douglas Debates of 1858
http://www.stolaf.edu/people/fitz/COURSES/debates.htm

LD Debate: NFL LD Topics
http://lddebate.org/files/ldtopics.pdf

Lincoln-Douglas Debate
http://www.csun.edu/~dgw61315/debformats.html#L-D

National Forensic League
  http://www.nflonline.org
The Writers' Place: The Toulmin Model
  http://www.writers-place.com/toulmin/sld001.htm

Index

B
Black's Law Dictionary, 13, 18

C
claim, 34, 35
constructive, 10, 21, 24
contention(s), 17, 19, 24, 25
criterion, 14, 15, 16, 17, 19, 24, 25, 27, 28, 29, 31, 32, 34
cross-examination, 20, 21, 22

D
data, 34, 35
definition(s), 12, 13, 16, 18

E
ethos, 35, 36

I
impact, 34, 35

L
logos, 35, 36

P
pathos, 35, 36

R
rebuttal, 21, 27, 29, 31
resolution(s), 9, 10, 11, 12, 13, 14, 15, 16, 17, 22, 29, 31, 32, 33, 39, 40

T
tagline(s), 17, 19, 35
thesis, 16, 19, 35

V
value(s), 10, 14, 15, 16, 17, 18, 24, 27, 29, 31, 32, 34, 37
voting issues, 31

W
warrant, 34, 35

About the Author

Cynthia Woodhouse is the Director of Debate at West High School in Iowa City, Iowa. She competed for Bettendorf High School in Bettendorf, Iowa, from 1994–1998 and has been coaching ever since. Ms. Woodhouse has coached students to the high school Tournament of Champions and the National Forensic League National Tournament, has taught at the National Summer Institute in Forensics at the University of Iowa, the Kentucky National Debate Institute, and the Communication Forum. She has met her greatest lasting friends through speech and debate and looks forward to a lifetime of forensics.

Photo Credits

Cover, pp. 22, 25, 28, 30, 32, 37 Courtesy of the National Forensic League; p. 8 © Getty Images; p. 12 by Cynthia Woodhouse; pp. 17, 18, 19, 40 © Shutterstock.

Designer: Haley Wilson
Editor: Kerri O'Donnell